A Day in the Life: Desert Animals

Arabian Oryx

Anita Ganeri

www.raintreepublishers.co.uk
Visit our website to find out
more information about
Raintree books.

To order:
☎ Phone 0845 6044371
📄 Fax +44 (0) 1865 312263
💻 Email myorders@raintreepublishers.co.uk

Customers from outside the UK please telephone +44 1865 312262

Raintree is an imprint of Capstone Global Library Limited,
a company incorporated in England and Wales having its
registered office at 7 Pilgrim Street, London, EC4V 6LB –
Registered company number: 6695582

Text © Capstone Global Library Limited 2011
First published in hardback in 2011
First published in paperback in 2012
The moral rights of the proprietor have been asserted.

Edited by Daniel Nunn, Rebecca Rissman, and Sian Smith
Designed by Richard Parker
Picture research by Elizabeth Alexander
Production by Victoria Fitzgerald
Originated by Capstone Global Library Ltd
Printed and bound in China by South China Printing
Company Ltd

ISBN 978 1 406 21959 3 (hardback)
14 13 12 11 10
10 9 8 7 6 5 4 3 2 1

ISBN 978 1 406 22122 0 (paperback)
15 14 13 12
10 9 8 7 6 5 4 3 2 1

**British Library Cataloguing in Publication
Data**
Ganeri, Anita, 1961-
    Arabian oryx. -- (A day in the life. Desert animals)
    1. Arabian oryx--Juvenile literature.
    I. Title II. Series
    599.6'45-dc22

Acknowledgements
We would like to thank the following for permission to
reproduce photographs: Alamy pp. 14 (© Photoshot
Holdings Ltd), 20, 23 glossary jackal (© Robert
Harding Picture Library Ltd), 22, 23 glossary hooves (©
imagebroker); Ardea.com pp. 4, 23 glossary mammal, 23
glossary desert (© Richard Porter), 15, 23 glossary grazing
(© Ken Lucas), 11 (© Francois Gohier); Corbis pp. 13 (©
George D. Lepp), 17, 23 glossary herd (© Steve Kaufman);
FLPA pp. 7 (© Philip Perry), 10 (© Inga Spence); Nature
Picture Library p. 12 (© Hanne & Jens Eriksen); NHPA
p. 21 (Biosphoto); Photolibrary pp. 8, 9, 19, 23 glossary
scrapes (Juniors Bildarchiv), 18 (Mauritius/Kerstin Layer),
16 (Mike Hill/OSF); Shutterstock p. 5, 23 glossary
springbok (© Johan Swanepoel).

Front cover photograph of an Arabian oryx standing in
sand (Oryx leucoryx) reproduced with permission of Alamy
(© Juniors Bildarchiv).

Back cover photograph of (left) Arabian oryx walking in
sand reproduced with permission of Photolibrary (Juniors
Bildarchiv); and (right) herd of Arabian oryx in Sir Bani Yas
Island, United Arab Emirates reproduced with permission
of Photolibrary (Mike Hill/OSF).

We would like to thank Michael Bright for his assistance in
the preparation of this book.

Every effort has been made to contact copyright holders
of material reproduced in this book. Any omissions will
be rectified in subsequent printings if notice is given to the
publisher.

Contents

Some words are shown in bold, **like this**.
You can find them in the glossary on page 23.

An Arabian oryx is a **mammal**.

All mammals have some hair on their bodies and feed their babies milk.

springbok

Arabian oryxes belong to a group of mammals called antelopes.

Springboks are another type of antelope.

Where do Arabian oryxes live?

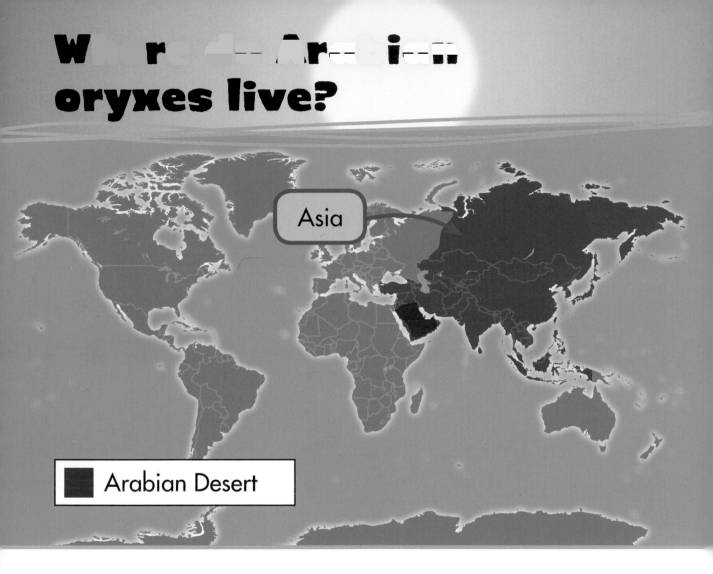

Asia

Arabian Desert

Arabian oryxes live in the Arabian **Desert** in Asia.

Can you find this desert on the map?

In summer it is very hot in the desert, but it can be freezing cold on winter nights.

There is very little rain in the desert.

What do Arabian oryxes look like?

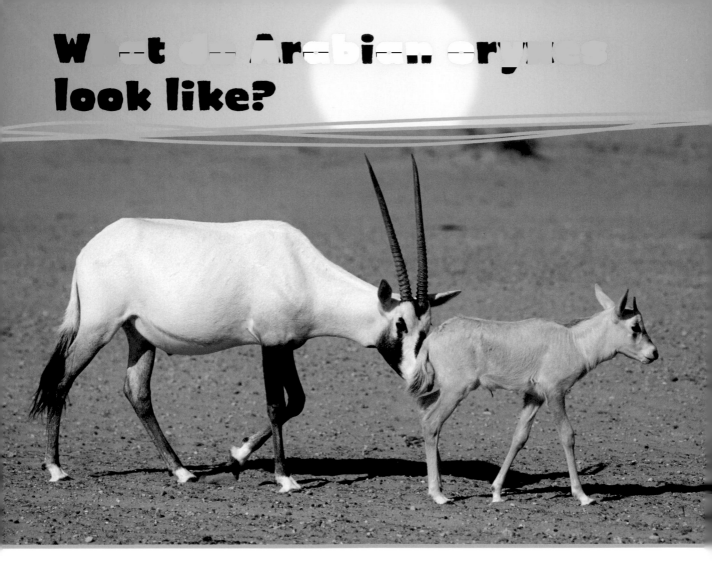

Adult Arabian oryxes are white, with brown legs.

Baby oryxes are brown all over when they are very young.

horns

hooves

Arabian oryxes have long, sharp horns.

Their wide **hooves** help them to walk across soft sand without sinking.

9

What do Arabian oryxes do at night?

Arabian oryxes usually start looking for food in the evening.

They spend most of the night **grazing**.

In the morning, it starts to get very hot in the **desert**.

The oryxes find somewhere shady to lie down and rest.

What do Arabian oryxes eat?

Arabian oryxes mostly eat grass and other **desert** plants.

They feed on roots, flowers, and leaves.

Arabian oryxes can go for weeks without drinking water.

They get most of their water from the plants they eat.

Are the oryxes stay in one place?

The **desert** is too dry for many plants to grow.

So some nights, the oryxes have to walk long distances to find their food.

The oryxes sometimes walk to places where it has been raining.

The rain makes new plants grow for the oryxes to eat.

Do Arabian oryxes live alone?

Arabian oryxes live in family groups, called **herds**.

There are usually around six oryxes in a herd.

When the oryxes move about, one of the females takes the lead.

The young follow behind with the male.

What do Arabian oryxes do in the day?

In the day, the **desert** gets very hot.

The oryxes stop feeding and look for a patch of grass or sand.

scrapes

The oryxes use their **hooves** to dig dips in the sand, called **scrapes**.

Then they lie down and rest until the evening.

What hunts Arabian oryxes?

Jackals hunt and eat baby oryxes.

A few oryxes are hunted by people, who eat their meat and use their skins for leather.

Arabian oryxes died out in the wild because so many were killed by hunters.

Some oryxes were born in zoos and put back into the wild.

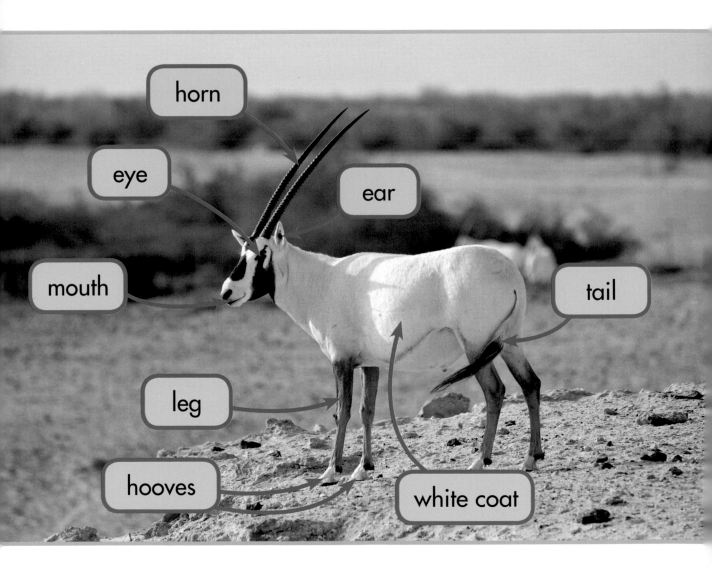

horn

eye

ear

mouth

tail

leg

hooves

white coat